Take Three: 3

DATE DUE

AGNI is known for its strong commitment to publishing both established and upcoming writing talents. Founded by Askold Melnyczuk in 1972, AGNI has published poems, essays, and short fiction by American and international writers including Seamus Heaney, Margaret Atwood, Noam Chomsky, Yusef Komunyakaa, Derek Walcott, Susanna Kaysen, Robert Pinsky, and Sharon Olds. AGNI is dedicated to bringing voices together in a magazine Joyce Carol Oates says is "known for commitment not only to work of consistently high quality but to thematic subjects of crucial and lasting significance." *Take Three: 3* is the third in an important annual series designed to launch the work of young poets chosen by AGNI's editorial board. *Take Three: 2* featured the poetry of Susan Aizenberg, Mark Turpin, and Suzanne Qualls, and *Take Three: 1* featured the poetry of Thomas Sayers Ellis, Larissa Szporluk, and Joe Osterhaus.

Take Three: 3

AGNI New Poets Series

GRAYWOLF PRESS

Publication of this volume is made possible in part by a grant
provided by the Minnesota State Arts Board through an
appropriation by the Minnesota State Legislature, and by
a grant from the National Endowment for the Arts. Significant
support has also been provided by Dayton's, Mervyn's, and Target
stores through the Dayton Hudson Foundation, the Bush Foundation,
the Andrew W. Mellon Foundation, the McKnight Foundation, the
General Mills Foundation, the St. Paul Companies, and other generous
contributions from foundations, corporations, and individuals. To
these organizations and individuals we offer our heartfelt thanks.

Published by Graywolf Press
2402 University Avenue, Suite 203
Saint Paul, Minnesota 55114
All rights reserved.

www.graywolfpress.org

Published in the United States of America

ISBN 1-55597-282-9

2 4 6 8 9 7 5 3 1
First Graywolf Printing, 1998

Library of Congress Catalog Card Number: 98-84458

Take Three: 3 was supported by a grant
from the Eric Mathieu King Fund of
The Academy of American Poets.

Jennifer Barber

Vendaval

JENNIFER BARBER grew up in Massachusetts, attended Colby College in Maine, studied medieval literature in England as a Rhodes Scholar, and completed her MFA from Columbia. Her poems have appeared in many journals, including *AGNI*, the *Georgia Review*, *Partisan Review*, *Poetry*, *Shenandoah*, and *Verse*. She currently lives in the Boston area and edits the literary magazine, *Salamander*.

to Pete, Jeff, & Zoë

vendaval: gale, windstorm, wind from the sea

I

Storm at Sun Up

The garden grows frantic
with the scratch of wings
abandoning the pear
      to vendaval, whose moan

is almost human
which is why the wives
have sleepless nights
      and the children

wake more than once.
Dozing in his yard,
the rooster takes the storm
      as something against him.

The bleary hens, still dazed,
rattle their alarm
too early, too late
      to be of any use.

The sun is up. The wind
is blowing and blowing.
Hung up next to grief
      with wooden pins,

a skirt whirls over
the skirts of lettuces,
sensual and sheer, half
      fastened, half undone.

Equinoctial

Wind that brings no rain,
raining down
chestnuts and twigs,

wind spiraled in the ear of fall,

the streets are listening
to the leaves swept above

houses, and the trees
with dust-colored birds.

I hear the tongues
rocked among high branches

and see the banner floating
from your open mouth:

wind that is both courier and path.

A Village I Love

It's stony enough. It's bitter enough.
A boy with a goad in the field
      keeps an ox and plow in line.

Vines cover the window of a shed
like an eye sealed shut by scars.
      Clothespins start clicking

when the wind takes up
whatever the mind won't touch.
      Widows are widows here, they hang

their tears to dry, they have the time.
Magpies on the garden wall
      chase away the smaller birds,

proving they are needle-eyed
masters of all they see.
      They see sudden shifts of light

followed by sudden rain.
Wind mutinies against the plow,
      the boy's dirt-caked shoe as he

takes a rolling step. I let the wind
snatch his breath and blur my eyes
      with his eyes, watching how the field

bends in on itself, his steps
swaying ground and furrow to the grief
      that sees what it holds, holds what it sees.

Nights

No one here dreams louder
than the wind, knocking

at the doors
where Franco's men

conscripted farmers' sons
fifty years ago for war. The wind

blows over strips of farms
no wider than a pony-run

and rivers made of
diphthongs, like the Eo,

and through the greedy
heads of eucalyptus trees,

the bearded, maimed
pines, through villages

whose steeples are crowned
with absurdly large

stork nests, set awry.
After a card game in the bar,

the men scrape back their chairs.
They leave in twos and threes.

Children and grandchildren
have moved away

to cities farther south.
They are all that's left,

a knock at the door
and the wind's long memory

of a bloody mountain pass
elbow-deep in mud.

Vaseful of Wild Roses

One crumples from five corners, dark
pink dissolving in white pink.

A long bud lets a petal fall
like some early sacrifice
to the indoor light. The eye, a vase,
can't keep the flowers whole.

The shape we know as rose
is their undoing: they
pass through it without stopping for
the word to form. They lean

toward us and away, as if
we were the wind and rain
and the reason they let go.

Canta la Gallina

The mulberry trees have been robbed
    of all but the last few
        rotting berries

at which the small birds work
    in a wind that blusters through
        the hen's brown-over-white

feathers, her peaked cap.
    The noise in her throat is not
        singing—yet it is

a mournful love of syllables
    that startles—she is out
        of the darkness of her house

to cross the yard like a ship.
    Rain blows warm and long
        over the loose tongues of grass.

Port Meadow

Port of nothing, where
a hundred white birds
break from the canal.

Where grazing land adjoins
the canal, with its lock-keeper's house,
the narrow boats
maneuvering the sudden bridge.

Where it is always Sunday,
always afternoon,
and those who are strolling
step around the swan's nest on the path.

Where you reach for my arm
and the beginning ends
with the sound of her name
in your mouth, two syllables.

Where the water glazes
the meadow after a rain
and there is a sail rising behind cows
or the silhouette of a horse
as water hens fly up
from the flooded meadow.

Vendaval

The brown hen is blown
toward the chopping block
and the red-handled axe.

The sea is rubbed bare in spots,
the sky El Greco blue
between the forking clouds.

The only gods are seasonal:
the holding back, the giving in,
the mistimed caress

against, not with, desire.
The wind dies as abruptly
as it started yesterday.

The day's late light
falls on us, unequally—it
makes a new map

of the blue bedspread,
luring disappointment
from our eyes and mouths,

letting us begin again.

II

History of Love

A gray and yellow bird
in the lower right
corner of my window
tests the pear tree, tests

the cabbages, and flies
to the tin roof
of the henhouse where
garbled cries are heard

at odd hours of the day—
the rooster wracked by doubt,
the hens in a darkness
darkened by the slit

of light admitted to the straw
and guarded by the hoe
whose finger scraped
the garden clear of leaves

yesterday, where a cat
casual, alert, curved
toward the henhouse door
and found itself looking in.

Letter

The letter unwriting itself
like a woman taking down her hair
      would explain to you
            what I am doing here.

The textures of my day, with its loose weave,
the small exchanges that rankle —
            everything would be so clear
      you would have to smile.

The letter would be an opening: it
brings us to a tidal pool
      where mussels fastened
            to green walls barely stir.

I have no letter. All that needs to be said
dissolves as easily as the sea,
            never leaving a wave onshore.
      It is the failure I practice.

Today

My glasses, swept
from the bureau to the floor

during an argument.
The loneliness of me with you,

the anger that sees us
shaking, and shaken.

Where haven't we been,
what haven't we tried

with the lenses of our love,
myopic, astigmatic.

The street is flanked by lawns
and solidly built houses,

quiet and unquiet lives.
Forsythia, magnolia.

How can I tell
pollen from rain, the blur

of green edges burning off?
The new leaves

grown invisible
on the light-filled tree.

Quarrel

Take the curtains down,
take the windows too.
Saw the legs off sofas,
the bed, the crib,
chop up the kitchen chairs.
Blow away the roofs.
Leave the houses shuddering
with their worried
dolls in separate rooms.
Set fire to the carpets.
Let the weeds come in.

Retyping

All the things that have to be left out.
A slipper on the lawn, the moon

an egg in the branches of the oak.
The floorboards, the curtains, my husband's arms,

another man I loved. No one need know
how many times I've dreamed of him

when the wind's branches knock the glass
and seed pearls of stars come unstrung.

It's morning, our neighbor Margaret
sweeps the night's acorns from her porch

where they fell, blunted and tannic
like old tears. All the things left out.

Across the street, light in a bedroom window
presses the blind, a car idles at the curb.

The City We Left Separately

There is no bridge
straddling the river
as it flows from the harbor to the sea.

There is no bridge
and sometimes, no river.

Boys run swerving at a pigeon
spreading its wings above their stones.

Nights are lost in
the alleys, the ringing phones.

There is no table, no chair,
no window opened
wide to summer,

no one sleeping where you were.

A Vermeer

Her earring a pearl,
a tear, if tears
were sheathed in nacre.

She is turning
to memorize
his leaving,

becoming what is
left to her,
his face already

painted out,
gone from all
but her gaze

and the oval
pearl loose on its wire,
about to drop

through the stunned
centuries
before she can deny

her longing,
which will last
longer than the slow

flowering of courts
and the brisk
blood of revolutions.

The Courtesan

This is one of Utamaro's
in a brown and red kimono,
her head bent forward on its stalk.

She broods on my calendar
over the days of April,
holds a brush already inked,

a thin horizontal:
how to start the letter she
should have finished months ago?

The kimono pools
around her flowerlike
ankles where his kisses fell.

He will come back to her
like a single, brushed word
floating on the page.

III

Summer as a Large, Reclining Nude

These are the days when summer lies
naked on the lawn, indolent and hot,
careless of the sparrows on her limbs.
In the freckled grass, you hear her yawn
deep within the pleasure of her mass,
giant breasts, belly, thighs and knees,
pockets of moisture soaking in the sun.
Across the street, a radio drones on,
describing the rank and file of two armies
dragging their equipment to the line
though a war seems far-fetched this late
in August. We're sleeping in the fear
of infinitely heavy arms and legs,
weeks defying the measurements of Thoth.
The rose nude yawns, rolls over in the grass,
draws us closer with a gorgeous laugh.

Daylilies

The buds are rolled parasols.
They wait for women to open them,
to stroll in sandals
and loose dresses
past the lost yards.

The stamen arch
forward in the flower,
hot little match heads
dusted with sulphur.

Under the eaves of a sleeping house,
desire is loneliness,
dividing what has been
from what won't be.

The orange silks
are longing to be darker.
They stand like flames
from the tall green wicks.

San Miguel

Lying in each other's arms
with too few or too many plans
      for living out the borrowed year

we don't ask what we're doing here,
the first year of our marriage. Here
      the days are bright, the grass

beyond the washtub gleams
like finely blown strands of glass.
      At night we have no visitors,

no witness but the night, the moon
leaning back against a cloud
      as if she couldn't bear this quietness.

Table

Give me oysters, the purple and green
puddle in each shell, their rough white rims,
the plate where they gather, skiffs
on a pond. Everything simple: the stocky,
reassuring knife, the lavender pitcher,
lemons blazing beneath their skins
on a blue mat, the blue mat on a larger
square of pink bordered with red,
red to the limits of the field
of vision, and beyond: this is the feast I need.

Second Child

We make love, knowing it's too late.
Nothing has started in the dark,

no murmur or clot of cells,
neither an eyelash or a fingernail.

Too late for her, imagined
daughter with dark hair and eyes,

forever out of reach, afloat
inside the water of sealed stars.

95° F

Here, in the center of July,
buttocks and large thighs are ripening
beyond the contours of their form.

The lovers can't lift an arm
without a drop of sweat that beads
the softened crease behind their knees.

The bed admits their trespasses.
Minotaur and bride, they grunt
in unison, as treacherous

as this heat that forces us
to wear his jowls and her lips
inside a Persian miniature

of rose and lemon, musk more pure
than all their straining to dissolve.
Separate them, and you'll see

how long an afternoon can lie
unwinding in the light
and how the lovers have become

enormous in our listless room,
their fingers cramped from lack of salt.
But evening, steep and cool,

lets the lovers leave
their persimmon flesh in place.
Summer has released us into sleep.

Copper Beech

In the crown of the copper beech
there are rooms
gliding along gray corridors,
the stone-smooth trunk and branches.

Sunlight wavers through
the warm air
of the inner ear,
a sound taken up in the leaves,
copper, red, a darker, older red.

The blood stirs softly
like the spread of fans,
black in the shade, red velvet in the light,

opening the rooms that have been closed
all this time, drawing me in
where light is the underside of light.

The Blue Dress

I slept and slept

as if Caliban had rolled
the boulder of his body onto mine,

and I could breathe,
breathe but not move.

I couldn't shake the stupor off.

Weeks floated like drowned bees.

If there had been a shipwreck,
if I was missing something
small beneath the waves,

I didn't want to look, I
        didn't want to say.

            *   *   *

The dress I bought
        for larger months,
blue dress with feathery
        white flowers on green stems,
                two pockets in the front:
        I'm emptied, empty

imagining loose petals
        on unwinding stems
now that I have bled too much,
        now that spring and summer

won't make any difference,
the infant tissue lost.

Summer has grown old in me,
a loose dress, hiding nothing.

Photograph of My Mother,
A Girl in Central Park

The squirrel is so thin
it must be the Depression.
There you are, feeding him,
wearing a little fur-trimmed coat.

Mother and Father have
made you take your glasses off.
This is the only point
on which they agree.

Unhappy little girl, you smile,
conscious of the camera
as you reach a hand
toward the squirrel on the bench.

Your other hand is clenched.
I have to see, sixty years later,
if you'll open it, if you'll knock,
an orphan at my door.

Six Brightnesses

1

The grass is dry, the long
end-of-summer wind is here.

A child in the park
squints as he slides
down the slow metal slide.

The air is bright all afternoon.

There's no one at the taxi stand,
no taxi, no passenger.

The wind at the end of the street
asks a woman and a man

to embrace, to pull away.

2

Early falling nights
grip the houses and let go.

Unlatching
the gate to his yard,

a boy's posture resembles
the posture of his father,

shoulders slumped, head down.
The clouds he doesn't see

are brighter than
the moon he doesn't see.

3

My father gave me
the sadness of his childhood,

my mother, her stubbornness
and her scrubby hair.

I want to grab her arm
and tell her what I see:

a weed at the edge of my yard
growing with such force

from midsummer on

so that by August its leafy stalk
towers over everything

and the pale blue flowers bloom

in a bright neglect,
wild, overlooked, at home.

4

A church stands by a synagogue,

a widow in black
passes a teenager in black,

the brightness of glass balconies
dazes the cobblestones

as blue pigeons rise,

a woman and a man
reopen the same argument,

it doesn't have an end;

a half-built apartment block
has to wait another year

for someone to work on it
or praise the windblown

patience of its rooms.

5

What will I give my son?

Which anger, which brightness

will tuck him in at night
in another year, will he

see through to the carpentry
in the stories I read him —

the poor miller's son
triumphs with his clever cat
and the barren fields revive —

or will he listen to the wolf
of his own imaginings
that turn him inward on himself

in his dark moments, how
will I keep him safe,

which story, which hero
sings the measure of his sleep?

6

What is done
remains undone

in the day's margins, at the end

of summer, in the slow

changes that overtake
a woman and a man.

This time they know
whatever love they've made

is as uncertain

as the weeds' laughter
in the wind's dry throat,

in a colder brightness.

Mark Bibbins

Swerve

MARK BIBBINS was born in Albany, New York, and lives in New York City. He received an MFA from The New School, where he teaches part-time. His poems appear in many anthologies and journals such as the *Paris Review*, the *Yale Review*, and the *Antioch Review*. He is currently the assistant to the editor of *The Best American Poetry* series.

Sinking

He takes night as a kind of medicine,
swallowing it with a buck and shiver.
Sometimes a drowning must come from within

and spread stealthily out toward the skin
with the drowsy patience of a fever.
He takes night as a kind of medicine,

his blood expanding as the moon goes thin—
its liquid light is something to savor.
Sometimes a drowning must come from within,

where it works like the fingerprint of gin
on the breath of an unfaithful lover.
He takes night as a kind of medicine

and relishes its pliable calfskin
smack, hoping it will blunt him forever.
Sometimes a drowning must come from within.

Finished waiting for the end to begin,
he's a thought in the mind of the river.
He takes night as a kind of medicine—
sometimes a drowning must come from within.

Halves and Half Knots

What slipped sorcery, what embarrassment
      of witches got this

wrong? So unwieldy, the business
      of enchantment —

when we say we, we are not who we say.
      An egg with two yolks

looks like luck to me, but I have
      been known to mis-

read. I want to
      call you

and ask you what it means.
      On the way

home last night, the stars were bigger
      than the city

and everyone had left their doors open
      so that they might breathe

such bright
      air.

Maybe that's what I meant by the trouble
      with magic — the night

has a frivolous sound without you here
      to hear it with me.

Just look—with all my yolks
　　　　in a row

and these half knots undone
　　　　I remain

capable of nothing
　　　　if not love.

Let Gone

after Paul Klee

As if this were the only catalyst, sufficient to
      leap endless work before us—rumors of
         bliss, the right light.
      Ah, that mouth, impeccable and silent
as a wish—someone has come up missing. Impossible
      now to trace when we heard footfalls, not just
         the echo of
      footfalls on the circular ramp. All we
have now is echo, and we've come to doubt what it was that
      made the sound to begin with. Admit it,
         we looked away—
      lost focus, let ourselves think something else—
for a second—it's how we lost him. Maybe a song from
      the afternoon distracted us, sugar
         straight from the box,
      a spreading ache. Someone implored, *Let him*
kiss me with the kisses of his mouth, and that was enough—
      we had to be squired away. Who spoke this
         will always be
      let gone. We could each of us set down his
glass of wine and sleep within a mesh of bliss, bright chain mail.
      Still, the echo—an urge for flight tempered
         by chucking blades—
      the air between them comes out palpable
as scar, a ration. I hear someone found his shoes, nothing
      else. Look at us, desperate for rumor.
         Still, one wonders
      if the noise might stop if we took the shoes
and wrapped them in a sheet. So often it is light that makes
      a tone unbearable. Who's absent now?
         And who does not
      know that always another sound will step
forward?—here, the ringing of tin wings in the almost air.

Coelacanth

In the sweet black rubber
mallet of your gaze,

I felt cool, pacific rainfall
on my knees until

you gathered your scales,
weathered asphalt

shingles on an old house,
afraid they would fall

away. It has been millions
of years since you felt

the wound of losing
flowers to the water—

scarlet anemones—
full, expectant heart-scoops.

You know now to laugh
at the worst things

that happen to you, as when
they hauled you up

in the fatal air, whispering,
We thought you were dead.

Don Quixote Cleans House

I am the dream soldier
who one night
with difficulty

maneuvered an upright
vacuum cleaner
upside-down and out

the window to see
if I could suck
down the sky

stars and all
but succeeded
only in startling

a few bats
black as burnt witches
who spun in jagged spirals

up toward the blood-blue
dome of a night
that always knew

how to evade me

Isla Mujeres

That faded sign, you know the one I mean,
      where the ocean lurches like a drunk—

      we can't read it, but rest assured,
what it says is not encouraging:

neither *only love is warmer*
      nor *best place for the moon.*

      Right now a woman is tucking
into a wonderful salad

on the other side of the island—
      it took the year for her to think

      of it again. Dogs race around
peeing on one another with aplomb.

At night everyone is warned away;
      they spend this time grasping

      for other words for blue.
Here comes someone else we will

miss and miss again—
      not that you're not staying here,

      but the village is clever,
even at rest.

Postcard with Small Letters, Summer 19—

A sea-blown haze mugs us with its weight,
      prompting underwater angels to
            bud and spill on the steamy pavement.

They rise, waggle their hair in the rain.
      Feeling around where their wings once were,
            they blush in their perfect nakedness.

Later someone radiant dances
      in place on a linoleum floor
            and has little to add. Radishes

doze in white refrigerators; we
      can hear the breath of animals, not
            our own. Our skin just now got closer

to the weather, and letters reread
      themselves. Always something new—although
            somehow red wine remains just the thing.

Christmas bulbs hang in the trees; one swells
      with light, escaping its wire: that one
            is the moon crooning in the low dark.

I wish you could hear the crickets—they're
      doing that trick where they sing with their
            legs, and things are beginning to cool—

            here is all of heaven we're allowed.

Charon Falls in Love

No one ever expected you
   to grow wings

or to step upon land,
   prowling the damp stones

with meaty feet. Nor
   were you wont to fall in love

and kidnap a passenger, say,
   some boy made myth-lovely

by death, and paddle madly
   upstream through the thick

and fishless water, coins
   flying in ghostly arcs

like fat metal moths
   from your ratty cloak.

Myth does not allow
   for such spontaneity, even

where the shivering waters
   of woe and lamentation meet

and seem to continue
   beyond the lip of the shore,

rising in spectral waves
   of pale asphodel.

Kamikaze

An open oven door
is the glass runway
upon which the pilot lands
after circling for years

in a contagious fog.
He has waited so long
for lights that would guide him
safely to the ground.

Everyone has disappeared
from this hollow plane,
though the parachutes hang
like bats asleep in rows,

dreaming of the sky.
This cave smells sweeter
than he had imagined.
Its air sounds like rain

falling through trees.
It helps him now to remember
that there is still nothing
easier than breathing.

The Parts of This We Remember

Without television, they might have been
no more than stolen coins left
on a railroad track and flattened,

making it difficult to imagine faces
with mouths telling us
that love is not a feeling

but a decision some people don't make —
and heaven is even better than peace.
In a laundromat in Manhattan

a Korean man stands bewildered
as he stares at his wet clothes
falling in circles behind the glass

like seaweed in a wave,
as if they might have an answer.
The owner of the laundromat is convinced

the Korean man will understand English
if he yells his words and repeats them.
There are men even worse than this

on the radio tonight, telling us
we need tougher immigration laws.
It is hard to think

of a building as being alive
until we see its entrails trying to close
themselves around a wound

and failing. We can almost see
the sky pull back
during the next few days,

affording space in which to die.
Somewhere, an Iraqi woman is driven
through the rooms of her house

by pale, stone-throwing hands
until her premature contractions
push a stillborn son

into the righteous Midwestern air.
No one says, "Bring us a picture
of this baby to put on our news."

When this, too, becomes mythology,
theologians will argue whether or not
an angel came to whisper in the ears

of people who needed to know:
*When you try to count the babies,
one will always be missing.*

The Pathology of Proximity

I stink to make you bitch
is as good a reason as any—

he can't see through pockets,
but then, that's the point.

He knows by now that keys
make a distinct music,

different from, say, two dimes
and a quarter. Ranting, he trudges

the middle of the avenue
in his pajama bottoms—

to have that much room to one's self—
the cars always go around.

Two kids argue on the corner
like actors picking parts

of scenery from between their teeth.
Once the idea of blue

hair belonged to old women
and everyone got along

just fine, but that was before
any of us met. Up there,

Midtown East hoists itself, dull
and lovely, into air thick as roux.

I push a shopping cart along
the bottom of the fusty river,

adding things as I go, removing
others to make room. Exhausting.

Here a box spring, a softball, a muffler.
They all want to go home with me.

As bubbles stampede toward whatever
light they can, a noise like *yet*

crackles with possibility, but is more
likely only some bird's beak

plunging after mercurial fish,
or a coin thrown in for luck.

Geometry Class

Mark is a fag scratched in blue ink
                on the surface of a desk, and true

enough. Trust letters and numbers,
                if not hands that form them,

geometries of loss worked out
                on cool green skins of slate.

Clap these woolly erasers together,
                inhaling ashes of a dead theorem

as they slide down rulers of light
                slowly to the linoleum floor.

Trust what lines do to each other:
                they are creatures lacking malice.

If Mark Opened His Mouth
So Wide He Fell In

after Joe Brainard

Would he be able to grab
the uvula in time, as
the imperiled heroine
in a silent film
reaches for the vine
over the pit
of quicksand?

　　　　　　Would he come away
with a little bunch
of grapes and stained
fingers?

　　　　Would he gag on his
feet and cough himself
into his hand?

　　　　　　Would someone hold him
in a Heimlich embrace?

　　　　　　　Would he find
what he was looking for?

　　　　　　　Would any biblical
or other literary references
be lost on him?

　　　　　Would he make
a new home in the white
city of teeth?

　　　　　　Would he make a sound?

How to Build a Caipirinha

Lime

    The greenest longings puzzle us
when we roll our skins together.
Nothing else can grow out of here,
we say such dour and senseless things.

Sugar

    The more you crush me, the sweeter
I become. Look outside—pigeons
burst into birds of paradise.

Ice

    On freezing seas a mattress floats
and we must provide the ballast.
How much easier it would be
if we could alter phase at will.

Cachaça

    Lick my fingers dry, peek under
my sleeves: there is always enough
for a glass—half envy, half fool.
Let us imbibe what connects us,
the sting of the ethanol stars.

Out of Place

The truant slugs traverse the hallway floor —
    what trickery of rain has brought them up
three flights of stairs? Their dwindling trails are more
    like tears, each one a flat, extended drop
that quickly fades and disappears. Tonight
    the damp and cold have found their way inside
our pre-war building, luring in these sight-
    less creatures, leaving tenants mystified.

How else to conjure you? — I always do
    when things are out of place. Your countenance,
once nearly mine, was always filtered through
    remorse. I don't suppose there's relevance
in circumstance made tender by default —
    your kiss a crystal shaker full of salt.

Whitman on the Beach

We sit on barstools,
two random flowers
at the edge of a pool,
baffled by our reflections
and by our thoughts
of how the inevitable
kiss goodnight will be negotiated.

When you get up
to go buy cigarettes
I imagine what it would be like
never to see you again.

Walt Whitman recited
Shakespeare to the cold
waves at Coney Island—
sonnets floating like rafts,
line by line, toward shores
on the other side of the world.

I settle for mumbling
a few lines I had
written about you
into my cocktail.

By the time you return,
I have finished the drink
and forgotten the words.
I stir the thinning ice cubes
to see if they remember. You should
listen to what they say.
This may be your only
opportunity
to hear what I think of you.

Legerdemain

You have shown me
that there is no trick

to sawing a person in two,
and that still

the heart hovers
in the space between the boxes

as they are pulled
apart and spun.

Only the heart, lit
by greased light, can see

its image in the mirrors.
Your smile is effortless now

and nearly real. You have others
believing that if you struck

the air with your hand
at just the right angle

horses would leap forth.
But do this for me instead:

when you are ready
to reassemble my parts,

make me into a centaur,
then feel how the air shakes

as my breath uncoils
restlessly in your ears.

The Difference between Autumn and Fall

That I would die of forgery was clear—
figure this as birth, a pile of dry leaves
        and me underneath.
                    The harvest
moon appears, bloated and sexual as
late vegetables in the farmers' market.

We are almost ready to use our hands,
        to take October for an oyster now.

Things built to lapse deride the sun's genius,
the height of distance only seals a plan.
                You exude pause.
      Something dark is due.
           Your first.
           Yours first.

      The yield we love best
we pull, don't let drop.

Even planes
               falling from the air
            at night
        like red leaves
                do so silently.

And all because once I let a boy ride
away with something of me in his spokes.
        Something I thought I could spare.

Bluebeard

I am not certain I love him
and if I do
I am certain I do
not wish to.
He has become
as acrid and infallible
as the clouds around Venus,
invisible to a naïve,
earthbound eye
cast heavenward
as dusk thickens into night.

He was a daring jewel
hanging over the mountains,
promising the comfort of
the first-star-I-see-tonight,
but when I flew to him,
he proved impenetrable
and lethal.
Still, I continue in this
foreign orbit that spun
us together into these rooms.

I wait for him
with sheets pulled up
to a face that faces the wall,
wishing I could
disappear from the bed
before he arrives,
leaving behind only a fading
patch of warmth
in the shape of my body—
a body his hands
will not remember.

I know I am not the first,
but I cannot find the others.
He will not even tell me
their names. I want to send
carrier pigeons in search
of these men,
with my story tied to
their pink and scaly ankles,
but I know the very words
would pull them down like rocks.

My notions of escape
wither each time he enters
the room and turns off the light.
I clench my just-brushed teeth,
watching his outline
grow thinner as his clothes
come off slowly in the new dark,
and the way he undresses
is the way
Bluebeard sharpens his axe.

By Means of Red and Green

All night was roar, the way a sound moves
        faster through darkness,

upending its intangible hues.
        But nocturnal charms

dwindle beside a kiss you left on
        the small of my back.

With answers leading, those traps of dots
        set for the color-

blind always catch what they intend to.
        Whether this will prove

to be true of you and me, under
        this light, I cannot

guess. Colors make their own rules—for us
        unenforceable.

Somehow they coax, urgently as tongues,
        a thing like meaning

from the crevice between our bodies
        and will not let me

sleep. Trains rend the air and I am shucked,
        raw with need of you.

Mud

Then we had just the pink carpet, the drugs kicking in, the flat soda. A *loner,* you called me, *by choice*—but that would only be part of the story—in fact, it took dozens of wrong choices to get here. Oh, what I wouldn't give right now for a little lesbian chic. It might help me to connect these dots, touch my nose with my eyes closed, say the alphabet backwards. It also might have prevented me from botching my attempt at the resurrection—or, more accurately, reconstitution—of a boy who didn't survive long enough to try the new medications (*undetectable levels*: it seems like a reasonable aspiration). Rumor has it that to burn is not to destroy, but to rearrange. Encouraged, I gathered his ashes, mixed in water, kneading my would-be Galatea recast as a boy. Be warned, the edict Don't Try This At Home applies here: what comes is not flesh, just mud. The carpet is still recovering—it provided the surface for an illicit tango with a guy who fancies himself the incarnation of personal style, an encounter which left me sucking poison from my ankle. After a certain point (determined largely by astrological means, as well as by one's choice of hair-care products) worry becomes unseemly, a false mustache you forgot you had on. While the others were shooing ghosts from the room with rolled-up newspapers, the shadows hurried down the walls, off to yet another of their secret meetings.

Counting

While you are sleeping
in a bed tethered to the wall
by the cord
of a nurse's call button,
I count my fingers.
They outnumber the days
you have left
to spend in this room,
so I busy them with
arranging the cards
from the people who want you
to be a teddy bear
with a sprained ankle
and get well soon.
Late afternoon sun
shines through the plastic bag
that drips you drops of morphine,
and the light comes out numb
as it swims up the wall.
At the end of her shift
we serve your favorite nurse
a daiquiri in a paper cup.
She props her stockinged feet
up on your bed
and you rub them—
on her right foot
she has six toes.
She tells us this
was how she learned
to count to twenty-one.
The laughing minutes
fall away from us

like cherry blossoms,
and I want us to glue them
back onto their branches,
but you're sleeping again
and I don't want to wake you.

Safe

The skin on your face:
a sheet removed
from a bed, washed

and replaced. Something
underneath is not
just sleeping.

No one moved it
but the dirt is
closer to the hole.

I have since tried
to find you,
to climb

the sky
between us.
I could tell you

it is safe
to come back, but
there is no one left.

Once I slept
at the sweet edge
of your breath,

but now a cold
wind pushes through
this broken room.

Day of the Dead

I sent you a dinner invitation,
        gave it to a mole who
tunneled to where you were buried, but he
        was drowned by sudden rain.
I went digging for him — my waterlogged
        envoy, mudbreather, shape-
shifter — and there, pinched between his yellow
        teeth, was your reply, wet
and bleeding on itself, illegible.

The shrimp are shriveled and dark in their blue
        bowl. One is curled around
the layered heart of a scallion like a
        small fist. They will not rise
up, pink and new, from this garlicky grave
        to dance with black beans in
the air above the table. There is no
        time for magic. There is
nothing — only these dishes to be done.

The next morning, scraping candle wax from
        the tablecloth with ice
cube and butter knife, I wonder if you
        might yet float through the door.
My mind is always shifting with the forms
        of what it most adores —
bodies tricked into turning on themselves —
        and if our dead *do* come
back, we must be prepared not to want them.

Tidal

Waves reach
     for the moon
with soft, salty hands
     and speak around
        my toes
     in wet whispers.
I am alone—
        the sandy-haired boy
     with the shark-
     infested blood has drunk
the deepest of waves.
His hand emerges
     like an undrowned fish
        in the glistening dark,
     until salt sings in my eyes
and the stars leak
     out of their tiny cups.

MARK BIBBINS

Blind

There was no dawn today.
Rain on the windowpane
waits to be licked clean
by sun that forgot to shine.
Outside, your voice rises

through a subway grate
and metal wheels shake out
a list of names. I wait to see
if I remember yours.
All I feel now is blue—a cliché

under any light, even none,
but I let it engulf me.
I scoop out my eyes
and offer them to you
in a darkened theater

where a puzzled audience
whispers at an empty screen,
and I start to inch back blindly
toward the arms and mouths
from which I have fallen.

The Watch

On the floor
next to my bed,
    your watch tells

time without you.
If it weren't here,
    would I still

have something
you would come
    back for?

I consider wearing
your watch to work,
    noting the difference

its weight makes,
dragging my finger
    over its face,

thinking of yours.
But I don't, and you
    won't be back.

This Garden Keeps Us Here against Our Will

As was the case in Circe's palace, we have
       no clue how long it's been.
       Beyond the metal fence,
hairstyles and cars evolve, and the world knits shut

its wounds without our help. We do not notice;
       no one is missing us.
       A roster of flowers
extends along the path, evocative tricks

on the tongue whose lush corroborations lapse
       into pricey secrets
       of opening and closed.
The grass is a carnivore of sorts, my sweet—

let fall all you thought was fixed. We too exist
       to be observed then chopped
       off neatly at the knees:
once you've given you can never give enough.

Transit

In a sloping field beyond
   reflectors that line the highway,
   deer gnaw at cornhusks exposed
after the long wait of winter.

Their eyes reflect our headlights
   as my father points the car
   carefully into the field
and turns off the engine.

They seem to measure us in the spaces
   between the movements of their jaws,
   even as we tentatively open
the doors and step out

into the cold spring drizzle.
   Soon enough, they turn
   and vanish, their tan flanks
fading into the darkness

like thoughts into sleep.
   They understand something
   about us we don't.
On nights like this, I am a boy

curled warm on the ribbed vinyl
   back seat of my parents' car,
   looking up through the windshield
at iridescent clouds that fly

from truck wheels spinning through indigo
   air soaked in a pale orange glow.
   I don't understand these songs drifting
back to me from the a.m. radio,

but the simple tunes are soothing
   and sometimes a phrase makes sense.
   . . . moonlight . . . feels right . . .
I have always felt safer in transit,

gliding smoothly through dark and rain—
   departure and arrival are only notes
   that sound better when sung
like the lullaby of motion in between.

Covert

The moon will cast no shadows where we land—
its beams confounded by sweetness and blight,
your gravity forbidden to my hand.

You stream out of my loosened fist like sand,
upward into the diminishing light.
The moon will cast no shadows where we land

as it glides over our heads—an unmanned
boat pulled along on the current of night.
Your gravity forbidden to my hand,

I worry that you may misunderstand
or navigate to a place beyond sight.
The moon will cast no shadows where we land,

but bears pale witness to your desire and
confusion: you say you won't, but you might.
Your gravity forbidden to my hand,

you finally offered your kisses, fanned
them across my mouth like strange birds in flight.
The moon will cast no shadows where we land,
your gravity forbidden to my hand.

Maggie Nelson

The Scratch-Scratch Diaries

MAGGIE NELSON was born in San Francisco. She has published a chapbook of her poems, *Pacific*, and a collection with another poet, Cynthia Nelson, entitled *Not Sisters*. Her work has appeared in *Hanging Loose*, *Ms.*, *New American Writing*, and *Urbanus*. She currently lives in New York City, where she has worked as the assistant to the editor of *The Best American Poetry* series.

Lucy

The first thing
we learned was
that we are
already in
decline. Our
entire time
one opulent
blink of
an eye. I
believe it,
even now in
the quiet dusk
when all I hear
is the faint
jingle of an
ice cream truck.
Hong Kong is
counting down,
Antarctica is
moaning in
tectonic exile,
our tears are
inevitable. We
are not the
carnivores nor
apostles we
claimed, our
upper hand won
not by natural
talent but by
our large,
somewhat
disastrous
brains. Great

chunk of skull
ravaged by
prehistoric
disease, its
eye-hollows ask
about the soul.
Where were you
this afternoon
when I woke up
alone? A woman
is a pianoful
of secrets,
working her way
up the greasy
totem pole.
Confess to it:
the flawless
test flight
of the moon taxi
cannot outwit
the coldness
of Lucy's bones.
Make no effigy
of the wind
when it sifts
through me.

The Municipal Frontier

Everyone was talking about the death
of Boss Tweed. And how Nathalie loved
a fried egg on a roll with catsup,
loved her Kewpie doll on a stick. How
Julius was always sick with a whooping
cough no coughball bottle could fix.
How a parrot shrieked in the gypsy hall
How they stretched Johnny's legs so much
the skin on the back of his knees tore
and he was fine but he had bow legs.
All the kids called him Bow. How
the shafts filled with bottles of silver
and rye, Bon Ami disinfectant,
Duette's Reclaiming Powder.

In the stoops now the women have breath
the color of fowl. They wander the mall
with needles hanging from their calves.
Cardboard lodgings go up at night and come
down by morning, when merchants scrape shit
off the stoops with sticks. And sell their
brocades, linens, laces, leathers for less.
Sidney's Underwear Co., Sam's Knitwear,
Universal Hosiery. Where *se fala Portuguese.*
Where shoes come in ostrich, crocodile,
lizard. Buildings are wrapped in barbed wire,
their windows filled in with bricks or
taped shut with purple paper. There's
a mattress of blue roses left in the rain,
a bonsai garden on a soft tar roof.
The poor howl into damaged payphones,
pick absentmindedly at their fingers,
leaving bloody turds. My friends!
I remember how his legs bent toward each other

like branches. A pile of children a pile
of bones. Meanwhile all these terrific bottles.
Their terrible sparkle. Oh Maria. It takes
some time for the light to change. For
each day to seem different from the rest.

The Posture of Departure

I was looking for clues
Pictures from someone else's wedding

Phone numbers on baby-blue Post-its
Her blondeness and her tallness

Some song lists. Then you come round
and say, Let's make love proper

if it'll stop you from snooping
around like this. I say, if you

can't kill it, notice it. It's
an attractive morning. What

I mean is, I'm attracted to it.
Fuchsia flowers hang from the wire

The day kind of plops out, like
tuna from a can. Nothing's quite

of this century, not this bodice,
nor all this fresh air. Nor she

in her pale yellow kimono
wanting attention and not getting it

making cruddy accusations
I forget them now, just as I've forgotten

the taste of expensive chocolate.
You can hug a dead body, but

you won't get much from it,
maybe a whiff of the mobile virus.

You're better off choosing
your fetters. I choose arms.

Wish

What kind of pain is it
that has nothing to teach?

I sit around all day
burning things.

Then ask you kindly
Lay me down among the persimmons

and fear itself.

Dream Triolets

1

Your tenure in dreams
is everlasting
Is a blurry morning
Your tenure in dreams
demands your revival
& my red-blooded reprisal
Your tenure in dreams
is everlasting

2

We were going to Africa
to draw on the breeze
to recline in a mosaic
We were going to Africa
Men I love were morphing
into women I love & trees
We were going to Africa
to draw on the breeze

3

He'd risen from the dead!
And brought strange gifts.
Cheese, pasta, a bottle opener.
He'd risen from the dead
which was really just a coma
(So he couldn't have
risen from the dead,
and brought strange gifts.)

4

I abetted, was victim and privy
along with the women who eat algae
The waterways were wide and variable

I abetted, was victim and privy
to your drinking of the dregs
of abandoned Guinnesses, which
I abetted, was victim and privy
along with the women who eat algae.

5

I had come quite a long way on my bicycle
Is there anyone here who can help me?
When I pump the tires they turn to suits.
I had come quite a long way on my bicycle
Brian can help you, they finally told me,
but Brian isn't here today. So I cried
I've come quite a long way on my bicycle.
Is there anyone here who can help me?

6

Oh Joshua, why'd you go mad
and lay out all the pretty paper
to dry, rice paper on the rocks
Oh Joshua why'd you go mad
Up by Three Wells why'd you
leave me that fancy letter
Oh Joshua why'd you go mad
and lay out all the pretty paper

Rowing

We row our boat into
the skyline, beyond industry
Simple passage, rubies
Relief from nothing

Roots along the bank
somber, the color of coffee
Mother, what have we lost?
Whose borrowed heart is our rudder?

So it comes and goes
What stake have I
Honey I forgot, it's
that simple

Wrath starts as a storm
and ends as a poppy
I've never seen water like this
I've never seen the sky

Motel Story

We were in the middle of something big.
The United States, for example. I
was in a new bed in a new room. We
had a key, something to misplace and find.
All night we had heard a banging next door,
of intimacy or imprisonment.
You coughed and I ripped psalms from the Bible.
We bled all over. The blood did not move
far. It clung to the drain, towels, tissues.
In the morning I watched you in the lot
pulling a suitcase from the trunk, half-dressed.
In my dream we stay alive. In my dream
we stay together. Outside in the lot
your half-dressed flesh moves like weather.

Morning in the envelope

I'm in the bathroom
shaving the monster
when I say, At least
I don't have your
children.

There's dignity in that,
and in moving money
from one part of town
to another.

I think I was in love with
how you took control
of the situation.

But the ruse is up:
the "invisible snake"
is an empty cage.

Lottery

From the needle shack
unaccompanied bliss

walks out in the form
of a dog barking at

a cat protected by Plexiglas
You've got to get rid

of the habit—
six Sweet 'n Lows

and leaving your wallet
open on the counter

This afternoon is sorely lacking
in sunlight. Scratched the putty

off my ticket, no luck
One belly-up after another

Itchy red hands, brown snot
Some side-effects I guess

A double-decker bus lurches
to a halt, jostling a tourist

trying to take
a picture of the big-ass

gray zone, the hum-drum,
the savage, I saw God

in the needle shack,
He said no, nothing.

Shiner

I wake up growling apples and dirt
naked and stretched under a barn sky
I cannot recall how I hurt my right eye

Arch of vessels gone grape under the lid
An army of red ants, a cast of shadows.
Good God. My eye has gone weak. Simply

put, I walked into an opening door.
The world is constantly changing shape
very dangerous. Two desert tortoises

duke it out on Arizona soil. By morning
one's always left belly-up to boil.
Now you roll around with a rock

and see what kind of bruise *you* can muster
Dolefulness, caprice, regret, trauma
My bicycle has two seats get on

Dramas

I

You're not my family at all
said the prodigal son
But this is dreamy meatloaf

There may be a pea stuck
to my cheek, said the patriarch
But I still wear the teeth
in this family

Yes you do, said his wife
Like a shark

(Enter hydrogen atom) I am simple
(Enter volcano) I am dormant in the corner
(Enter tulips) We are still on the piano
(Enter diamond) I am stable and elegant
(Enter attractive liquids) If we mix we'll explode

(Enter Buddha)
What am *I* doing here? And who
is the white kid with the red guitar?

(Prodigal son stands. He has the guitar.)
I came to fight, like a man

Gimme that champagne
said his brother
who was no longer boy genius

II

Take off that sombrero
said the whore to the caballero

(Caballero begins to remove her garters
with an ugly musket)

(Enter female soldier)
Hold it right there
Both of you

(Caballero exits. The two women smoke.)
The difference is, said the whore

You want to kill men
We want to make them happy
Now let me pin a great pink camellia
to your breast
Then you'll look
more like a woman

I see, said the female soldier
(She fingers the flower)
Thus becoming a more poderoso
revolutionary

Letters from C.L.N.

I had a hellish toll-line on my way
home from LaGuardia that day.
All that clutching is hard on my bad knee.
There's two thousand miles between you and me.

Doesn't it feel spooky now
to think of how we ran around?
The new Gorilla Lounge
is superior to the old one,

but it has no heat. Two
weeks into Prozac and sleep
I'm losing to the dogs. My sister
calls it "the trendy drug."

I was under the impression I was served decaf.
I'm really into the word "temperance."
I wrapped a book for my father
in a map of Nevada. The lines looked nice.

I still want you in tile, in leather,
in jewels. I still want to buy
a flash camera, so when you come back
I can shoot you in the dark.

Dear Sirs:

I include with this letter
my complete collection of

oval fronts which I have
been cutting from your boxes

for years. Your oblong
cakes of fairy soap

occupy quite a privileged place
amongst my toiletries. I look

forward to receiving
your generous free gift.

There is a statue of Neptune
which I am fond of visiting

whose feet and hands, alas, have
deteriorated from acid rain. What

is left of this ancient king
is vulnerable to vandalism—

He has already suffered the theft
of his ornate trident.

Something must be done!

My husband is much beloved.
He is not, however, a sensual creature.

How can I entreat him
to touch me, not leave me

amongst the piles of
putrefying furniture?

Well, this letter certainly
began in lighter spirits!

I apologize for my diminished
powers of meditation —

Yours Truly,
"A Dedicated Patron"

Villanelle to the Critic

*"These are not poems at all, and I feel that I have, without
right or desire, been made a third party to her conversa-
tions with her psychiatrist."*
C. GULLANS ON ANNE SEXTON

This is not a poem. What's more, I'm a liar.
It's a basket of illicit love, or beating yeasts.
It holds you hostage without right or desire.

The words seem raw and pure. But they conspire
to draw you into my severed head. You repeat:
this is not a poem. What's more, I'm a liar.

The stanzas and rhymes build only a wire
fence around an adolescent violence. At least
you keep your distance, your right, your desire.

Still you will try to find me. You never tire.
You have to dole out blame to feel complete.
This is not a poem. What's more, I'm a liar.

It's such a shame. This villanelle once aspired
to greatness, to pleasure. Now it is weak.
It says too much, without right or desire.

Take your pick: poet, patient, whore for hire:
any which way, you get to play the priest.
But if this poem confesses, then I'm a liar,
forever a fantasy without rights or desires.

Happy Hour

You get one, then
   you get another
The most important faces
   are the ones you can't remember

The gothic translucence
   of her blue eyes and teeth
Heavy blue, rich chianti
   Oh gorilla, temptress, stranger,

your exit now would truly be
   a betrayal. I am swelling
with lymph and a fatal
   radiance. It's just you

and me and artifice now, and
   I can tell you love my mind.
You get one, then another
   It's a place without color

It's a diary of space.
   Little green bills grease
the Catherine Wheel, the carousel
   of spices. If they were flowers

the erotics of tea
   would not be lost on me.
You really made a woman
   out of me. Before that,

I can't remember what
   I was—a cell,
a cuff, a girl. A piece
   of pure doggerel.

What it's come to

This must be my strap-on life
my weeping to all four corners.
Dull fragments of our future
roll loose in my blood. The thought
of it, a barnacle on the nerve.
One foot doesn't even feel like
following the other. I'm left making
snow angels at the pass. Love
that came too late, love that ate
the grave, love that had perfection
but began to ooze at the seams.
Will we ever move on with ease?
I am letting go of lives slowly
small animals I am setting free

56 Westervelt

We sat
in big
chairs
in front
of the
steeple
and the
sodden
street
curled
up in
morning
and in
love.

Before
character
sealed
fate,
magic
was simply
the un-
shakeable
belief
that
magic
would
happen
to us.

Sty Town

Wake to an August so mild and genuine
  New York is always right outside
It won't ever be like this again
  Great green summer of the mind
A row of men play chess in the heat
  As taxi cabs slowly circle
One quiet, resurrected street
  The sky is a nubile purple
And the air has the aroma
  Of a public pool. The day makes
Its misty slide into night
  And just when it seems too late
A woman will walk by
  Her name written in water

And we must take photographs of all this

Uneven staircases lead to rooftops
made of sloping and moist black tar
where we can see what we've done
so far, i.e., metropolis. It's still
"who's wearing the pants" versus
"no pants" versus "my mind is on fire!"
which may include dying tulips, a
mouse leaking on one side, lizard
music on late night TV. Aboard
the M15 a mother screams, "Don't
make me hit you in front of all
these people!" Then further back
I meet an Apache, he says,
"Can you believe it? A fucking Apache."

28

Please touch the tender
ink that once ran darker

Now runs softer
Touch the cells

held between thumbs
Body of perfume

Forest of swordfern
Nod to the schism

as we pass by
matches lit and left

on the landing—If this
is obscurity, so be it

We are bold, the sea
our choir.

'Love, if you love me'

Watching the seagulls turn blue
as day goes down on the austere city
Even the industry looks terrific
And so goes your agent of disrepair
The body that keeps denying
the comfort you're seeking
Still you try to love Wednesdays
as much as Tuesdays, try to build
things without using your hands
You cannot wait for grace to move you
but you can't move without grace
So of course you don't know
exactly *what* to do next
You pay rent for the March of clouds

New Year's Day

A drunk that lasted for two years
just came to. Got up,

looked out the window,
crawled back to bed.

Oh my friend, we've become
something else.

The parting of ice-nights
The acme of resolve

which quickens, transforms,
lumbers home alone.

Oh my friend, what's left
of love

is love.

January 27, 1984

Let me get the story straight.
He had gone to the ballet.

It had been beautiful.

He came home, sipped whiskey
and water, took off his glasses,

went to sleep.

He did not dream.
He did not get the morning paper.

He did not get the mail at three.

He did not get up to make dinner
and did not meet his evening date.

Earlier that day his ex-wife
had jogged to his house.

She had stood outside his bedroom window and wept.

She did not know he had died.
In fact she was crying because

they had divorced, and were still alive.

Later that night, as she tried
to rub heat back into his hands,

she understood what had come and gone.

There is no telling when a body
reaches its peak.

He did not dream, he did not shriek.

As far as I know the story,
he died in his sleep.

February

Not as glorious
as a gulf sunset
nor you with a
gardenia tucked
behind your ear
but different.
Things set out
on the sidewalk
A purple velvet chair
A skinny metal locker
But we won't want them
because they're wet!
Have you heard of
a cat abortion? Nor
had I until last
night. Peetie had
one and come to think
of it, Peetie isn't
a girl's name. There's
something awful about
mid-winter, and I'm
not talking about
people freezing
on their way to
the outhouse nor
stillborn calves
I'm just talking
about the way it feels
to put on the same coat
every day. Your eyes
smarting from the
sleet. I wish I were
having some rougher
sex but what is that?

Where's my mother?
In Chinatown all
the lights glow red
and I have no idea
what they're advertising
Sometimes if you
don't know a language
it seems entirely
naïve or sinister.
Would someone please
shake me upside-down
and let loose all
these pennies? People
are screaming on
the street, they're
not unhappy just
trying to get each
other's attention.
Last night a woman
walked buck naked
for three blocks
with a crowd behind
her and when they got
to Houston Street
they passed around
a ski cap saying
"A Dollar For The
Naked Lady?"
I stay up
half the night
listening to garbage
trucks and weird
thud!'s from apartments
where people seem
to be perpetually
rearranging.
Maia wore earplugs

in the tropics and
Elli wore earplugs
in the suburbs but I
don't want to be like
Maia or Elli. Baby
you left your matches
on my desk, but I've
stopped smoking! It's
weird to be in love
with a friend. It's
so inert. Sure,
it's aesthetic, but
it exists right where
aesthetics slip into
sincerity. The part
in my scalp is
soaked, the bus
won't stop because
it's limited. I have
no will-power but
plenty of will so
I guess that makes me
an addict. And if
these clouds would
part we'd be able
to see Orion,
the heavenly
hunter.

I lost something of my semblance

Spring is piss-warm and ambivalent
A trigger to the head I would have cradled
Are you full yet, rotten consciousness?
Your demise quickened by catering

The eyes of a monster-child looking
for a piece of fence to chew
The death (inevitable!) of your mother
Followed by phone calls to unavailable agents

Meningitis airborne in a cramped aircraft
The ruin of everything through rumination
A lifelong dream you could have just bought
instead of dreamt. The dust ruffle

flutters as an eerie wind tours the room.
Oh California, there's nothing more
to be said or done about you.

Lune

Side of the
road windswept
by wind ready
to yes
I will all
the while
dogs and scrub
lie between
us make me
a promise
you've never known
how to
keep my skull
plush a
lantern of corn
your habit
a mystery I
was made
to unravel completely
Do you
know what I
love? The
unqualified quiet of
breath and
its lack of
reasoning meet
me at the
corner then
further where the
dark organs
live in the
bustle of
a morning bereft
of activity

a golden paw
comes in
from the rain
to stroke
us its breath
hot forgiveness
as the circus
slowly makes
its way to
our town.

Harbor

Not quite at home in the world
and turning toward the terminus

Night-swimming with my sister
who stays back by the shore

The force that gets the body
out of the soul

What's personal is what you hold
in your hand

A bottle of catsup
The pour of green water

If I were to escape beauty
into the season of giving

I would give to the birds,
the sad, and the leaning

I would use simple language
to describe the forest. Failing that,

I'd find a piano.
Nickel body, nickel world

You are a figure illuminated
from behind by a light

The underbelly of sunset
The rattling of blue logs

The house is over. That is,
what you never went back for

has been loaded into a dumpster
A bridge is an arc of green lights

over black water. This is memory
weather, and I remember

the roof in summer. How it stood.
How we stood upon it.

Not Yet

What I can
see from here,
why I cared,
two bridges.
Backs of
buildings,
filthy shafts
in between.
Trees losing
what they've
been losing,
broad yellow
leaves. The
neighbor's
rooftop garden,
fuchsia reeds
clicking in
the wind, the
steady ping of
antennae, metal
on metal. A
lone thong, a
smoke-red door,
sexy dreams
from the night
before. A pigeon's
orange eye, its
fat purple neck,
white wings
flashing white
against the
brick edifice.
Ample sun, wet
tea bags, New

Jersey. My
unforgivable
ways. Who wrote
A. Loves Dominique!
on the tower
across the way?
Well, whoever,
good for A.

Palomas

I have heard the world is becoming less direct. Still I unload my peculiar verbs into the machine and walk out onto the dazzling street. A man is scraping the sidewalk. Wise old men in wheelchairs career into the future, the palomas flood the square. I want to tell you about this day, its neutralness, its unwillingness to be anything other than itself. The snow goes on and on, carries cornflowers. I draw a bath of yellow water and weeds. The tea I make is plain. We are beginning again. Some people don't ever begin again. That's a different kind of life. On the one hand, I will not let madness have you. On the other, who am I to stand in its way? My face is pressed against dank blue floorboards and even the roadhouse nails are soft. Someone has a hand over my mouth. On the day of the wedding I will pick up a coil of driftwood. Everyone does not want the same things. Do you know the woman with fins, who would swim to the bottom of the grotto no matter how green and cold? No matter if her lungs shrink, no matter if her mind becomes plant. Love in the roadhouse, love in the snow. Ideas start and finish in love. The pollen disperses to reveal the picturesque, which will carry us through. Today I am witness to an orgy of filthy doves. The prick of it may grow dull. There is something that cannot be broken even when we are. And I *do* feel betrayed, but I have to get off the train.

Acknowledgments

Grateful acknowledgment is made to the editors of the following publications in which the poems below first appeared.

Jennifer Barber, *Vendaval*

AGNI, "Vendaval"
The American Oxonian, "Storm at Sun Up," "Retyping," "Port Meadow"
The Georgia Review, "Letter"
The Journal, "Copper Beech," "The City We Left Separately"
96 Inc., "Canta la Gallina," "San Miguel"
Noctiluca, "The Courtesan"
Orion, "Vaseful of Wild Roses"
Pequod, "History of Love," "95° F"
Poetry, "Summer as a Large, Reclining Nude"
Shenandoah, "Table" from "Two Poets and a Painter"
Verse, "Nights" (as "Vendaval Again")

Thanks to family and friends for their support, and to early readers of these poems: Peter Brown, Fred Marchant, Rita Gabis, George Franklin, Judy Katz-Levine, Don Share, Susan Monsky, Robin Dash, and Peter Harris.

Mark Bibbins, *Swerve*

Antioch Review, "Covert," "Don Quixote Cleans House"
Apalachee Quarterly, "Charon Falls in Love"
A & U, "Blind"
Bay Windows, "Geometry Class," "The Watch"
The Berkeley Poetry Review, "Kamikaze"
The Boston Review, "Isla Mujeres"
Chiron Review, "Safe"
Excursus, "Tidal" (as "In Waves")
The Journal, "Let Gone"
The Paris Review, "Counting," "Legerdemain," "Sinking,"
    "The Parts of This We Remember"
River Styx, "Out of Place"
Urbanus, "If Mark Opened His Mouth So Wide He Fell In"
Western Humanities Review, "Bluebeard," "Whitman on the Beach,"
    "Transit"
Willow Springs, "Coelacanth"

"Sinking" is for Liz, Robin, and Simon.

"Blind" is for Derek Jarman.

"The Parts of This We Remember" is for Salaam al-Saidi, who on April 20, 1995, was stillborn at seven months when citizens of Oklahoma City stoned his parents' house.

For their kindness and encouragement, Mark thanks Richard Howard, Scott Hightower, Susan Wheeler, and David Lehman.

And, of course, his family and friends.

Maggie Nelson, *The Scratch-Scratch Diaries*

Hanging Loose, "Not Yet," "The Posture of Departure," "February," "Palomas"
Urbanus, "The Municipal Frontier"
New American Writing, "Shiner"
Ms., "Motel Story"

"Letters from C.L.N." and "Motel Story" also appeared in *Not Sisters* (Soft Skull Press, 1996).

"Villanelle to the Critic," "January 27, 1984," "Shiner," and "Letters from C.L.N." also appeared in *Pacific* (Orchard Street Press, 1995).

Thank you: Lily Mazzarella, Cynthia Nelson, Suzanne Snider, Jennie Portnof, Edward Morris, Eileen Myles, Ross Fiersten, Noah Leff, David Lehman, and Askold Melnyczuk for their insight and assistance.

This book was designed by Will Powers. It is set in Charlotte and Franklin Gothic type by Stanton Publication Services, Inc. and manufactured by Bang Printing on acid-free paper.

Cover design by Jeanne Lee.